T0144956

A
Young Cherub, Trying to get Bigger,
<u>And</u> stronger, walks down a Fresh,
New, Never touched path.

Lets See what Things
We Can Catch!

To order additional copies of this book, contact:
Xlibris
1-888-795-4274
www.Xlibris.com
Orders@Xlibris.com

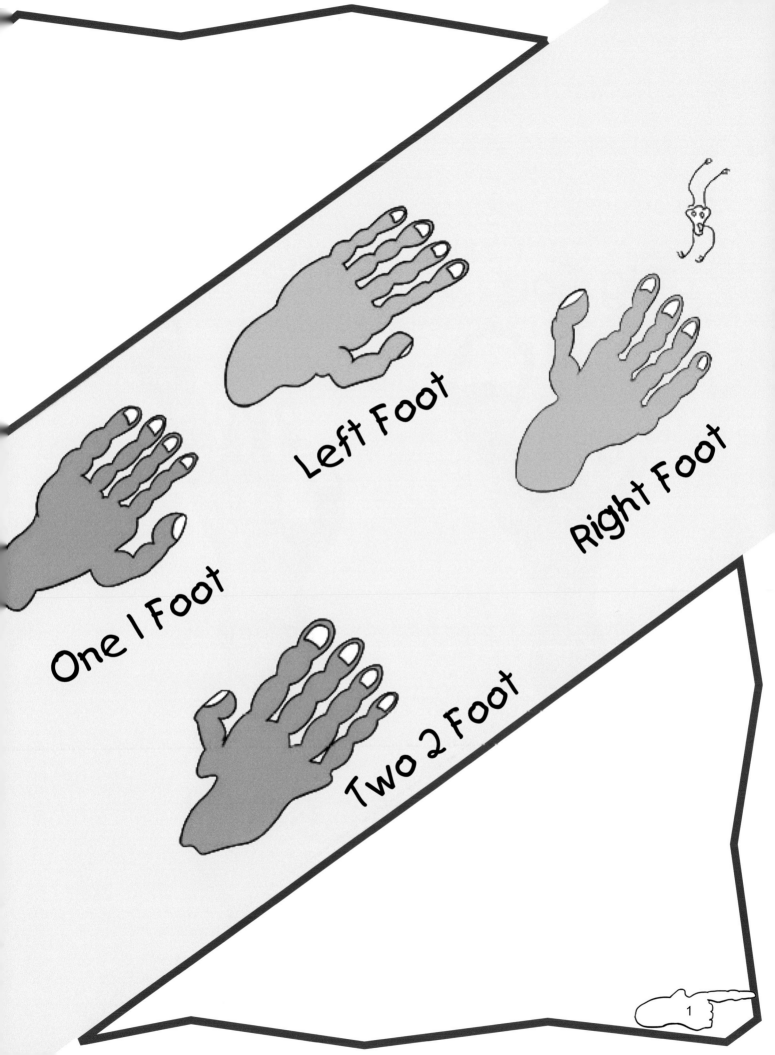

Big Toe   Little Toe

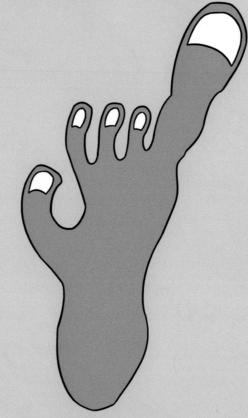

AND I USE BOTH
TO GO

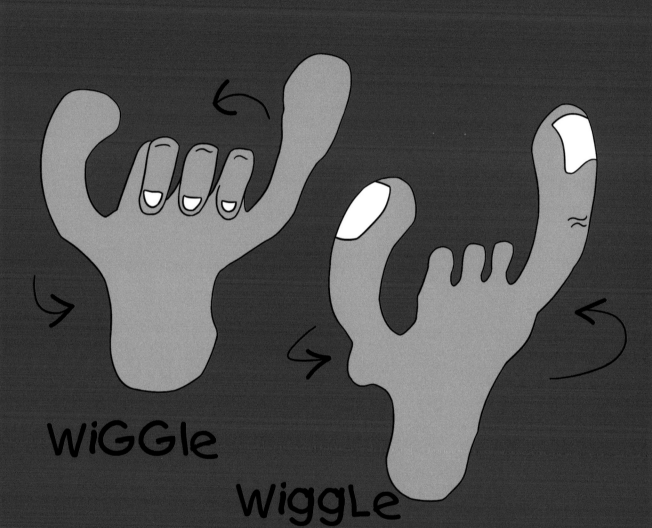

One 1 Finger

Two 2 Fingers

Three 3 Fingers

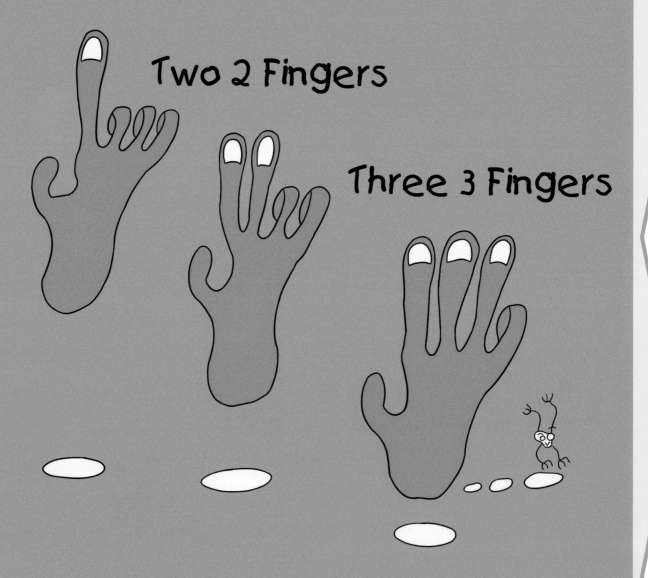

Why Does My
Right
H
A
N
D

Look Like My
Left
H
A
N
D

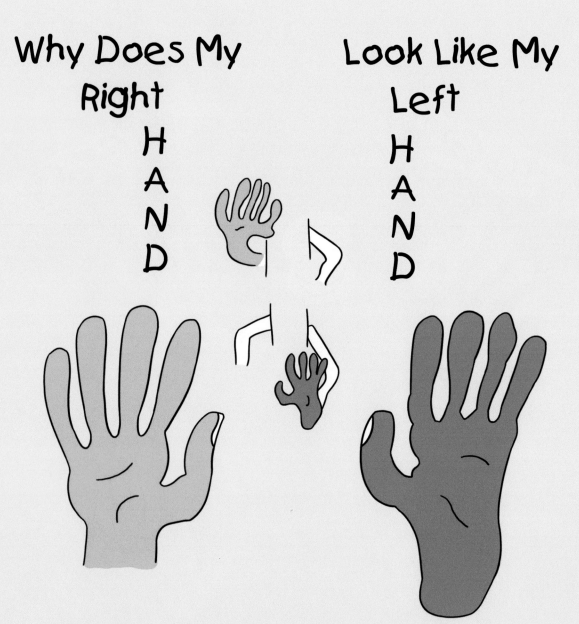

Can They Do what my
Other Two can? .. I Bet!

Wiggle Wiggle

WiGGLE

WiGGLE

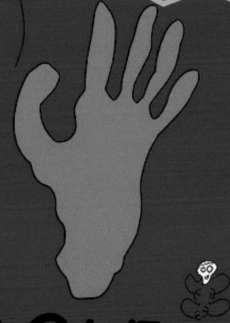

WiGGLE
WiGGLE

Now! What is that Pointy thing?

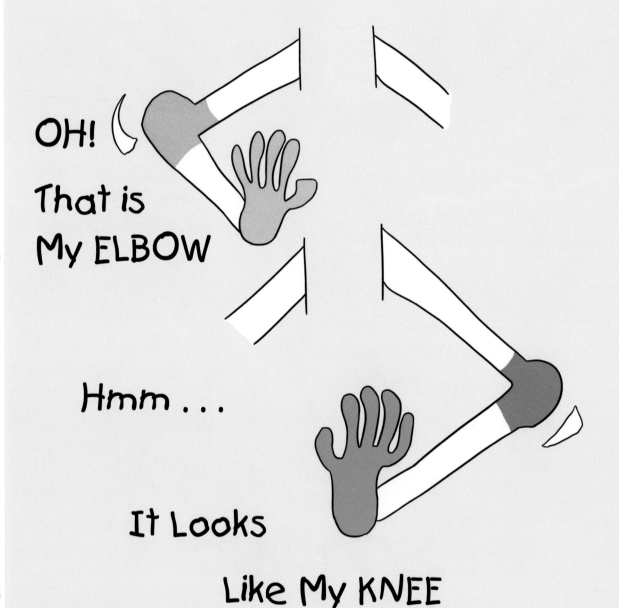

OH!
That is
My ELBOW

Hmm . . .

It Looks

Like My KNEE

Circle By Circle

I Watch THEM

GO

!CRAZY!

WIGGLE WIGGLE WIGGLE WIGGLE

Playing with Your Joints, See How Fun this is!

I Have Even

20 Little Ones

that Can Do

the Same

Things !

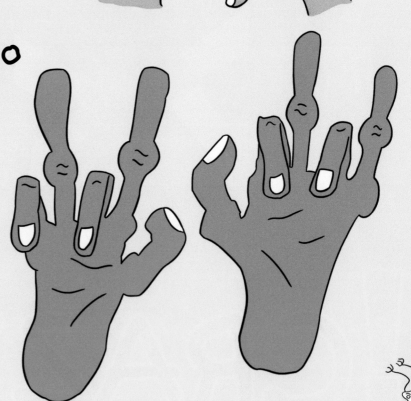

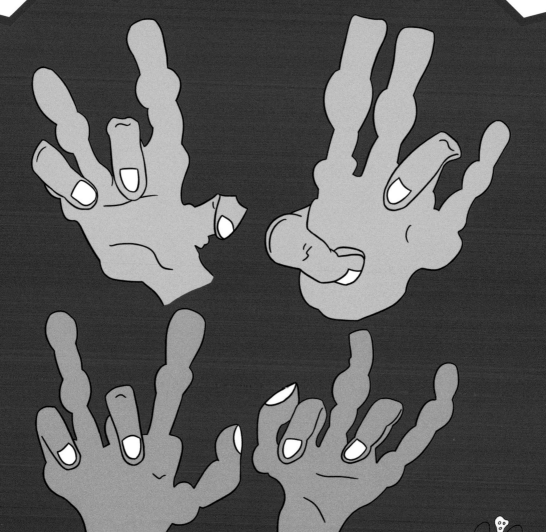

Hey !
My SHOULDERS Are Joints Too!

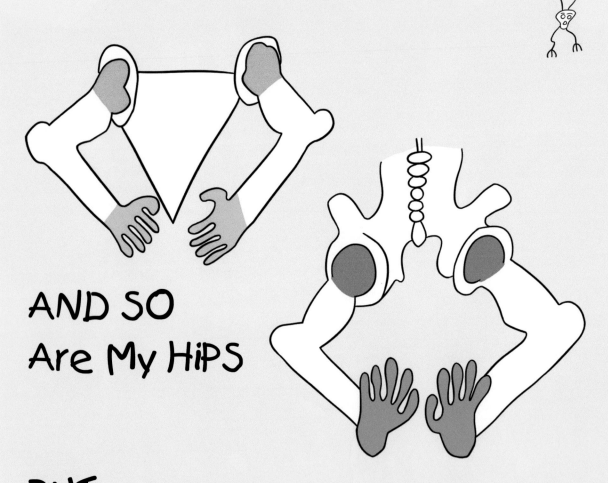

AND SO
Are My HiPS

BUT,
It Seems I Do Not DO CiRCleS
With them, AS MuCH AS My
ELBOWS And KNEES GET!

WIGGLE
WIGGLE

Wiggle

Wiggle

Oops.. Now there is One We Almost Forgot !

I Wonder What twisty Joint, WE LEFT OUT!!

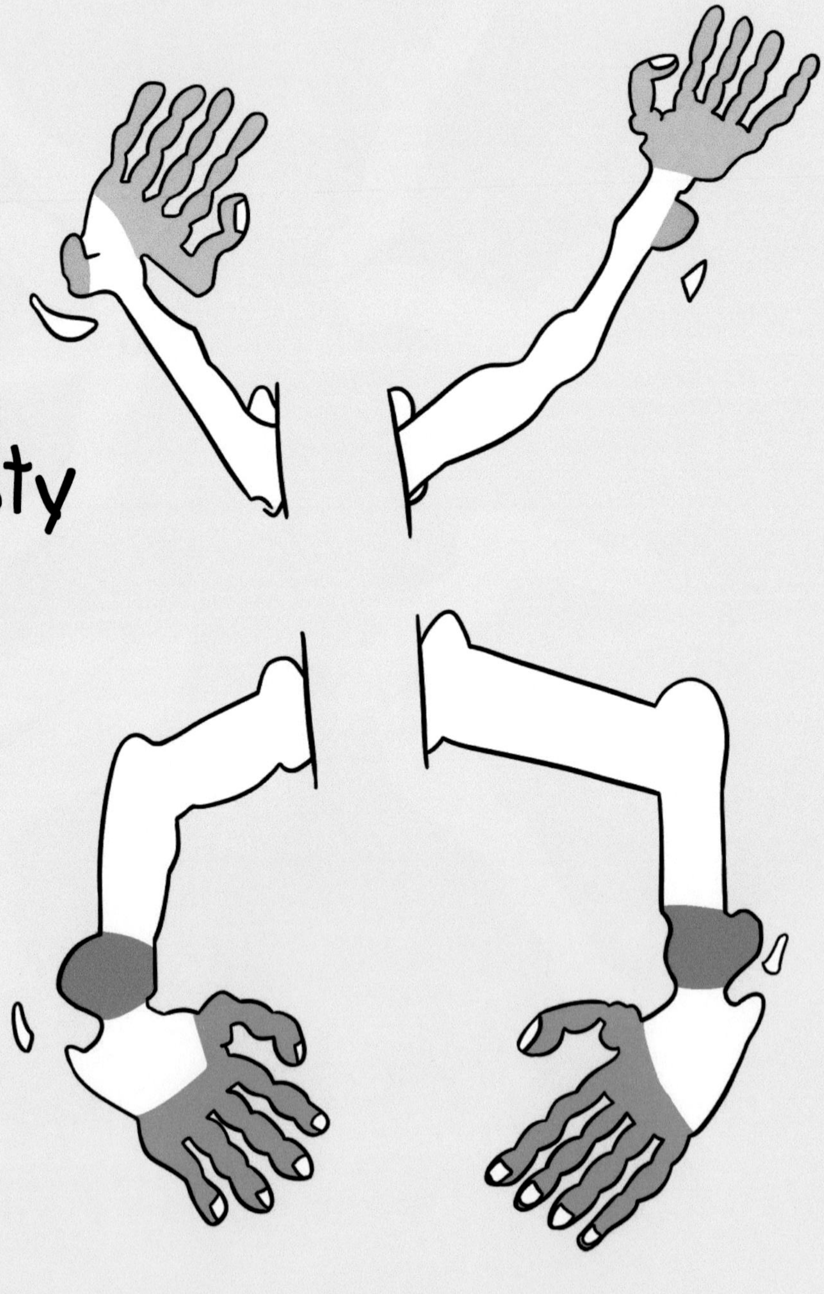

DOES ANYBODY KNOW ??..

These are My ANKLES!

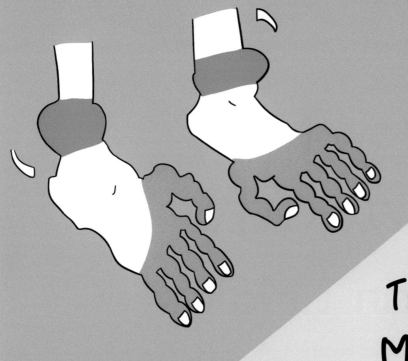

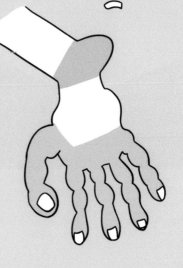

And These Are My WRISTS!

How Many
WIGGLES
can I Make
Them Get?

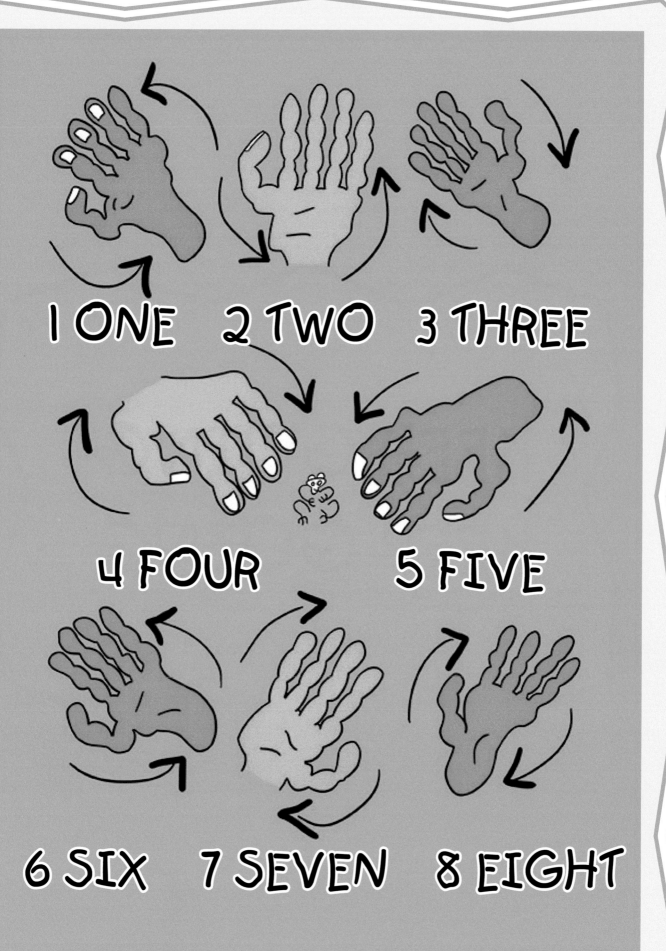

1 ONE　2 TWO　3 THREE

4 FOUR　　　5 FIVE

6 SIX　7 SEVEN　8 EIGHT

KEEP GOING
KEEP GOING

It

MAKes ME

BIG,

StronG,

AND

HELPS

ME

My FEET ARE My HANDs,

AND My HANDs ARE My FEET

AND Just Because I Walk On 2 TWO

Does Not Change I ONE Thing

NOW
We Are Ready,
AND warmed up to go

Down New Beaten paths,
With more fun to Bring to Show

Printed in the United States
By Bookmasters